Butterflies and Flowers

Adult Coloring Book
By Annabella Shaw

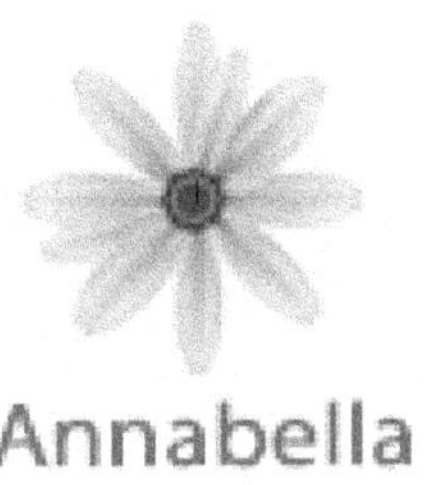

Annabella

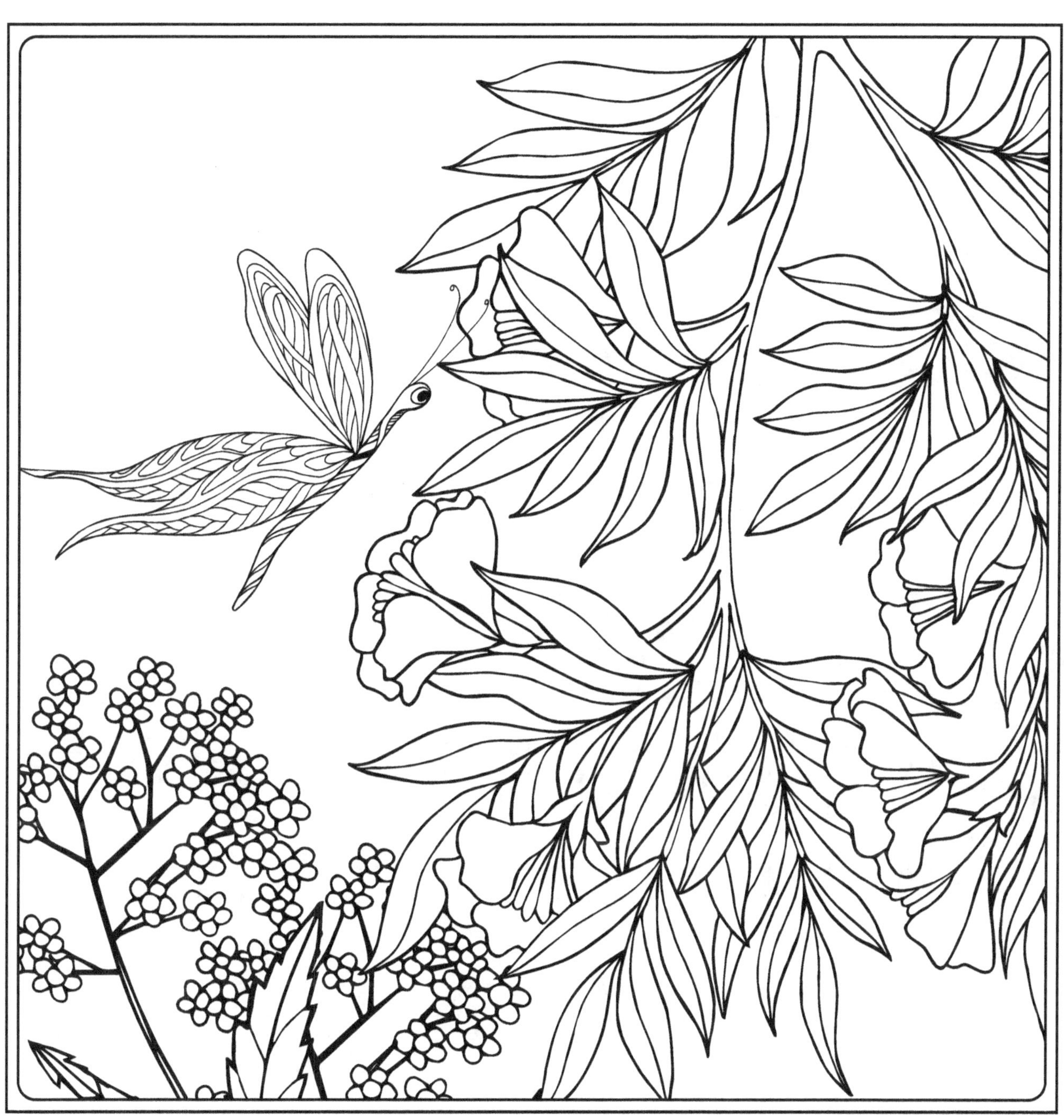

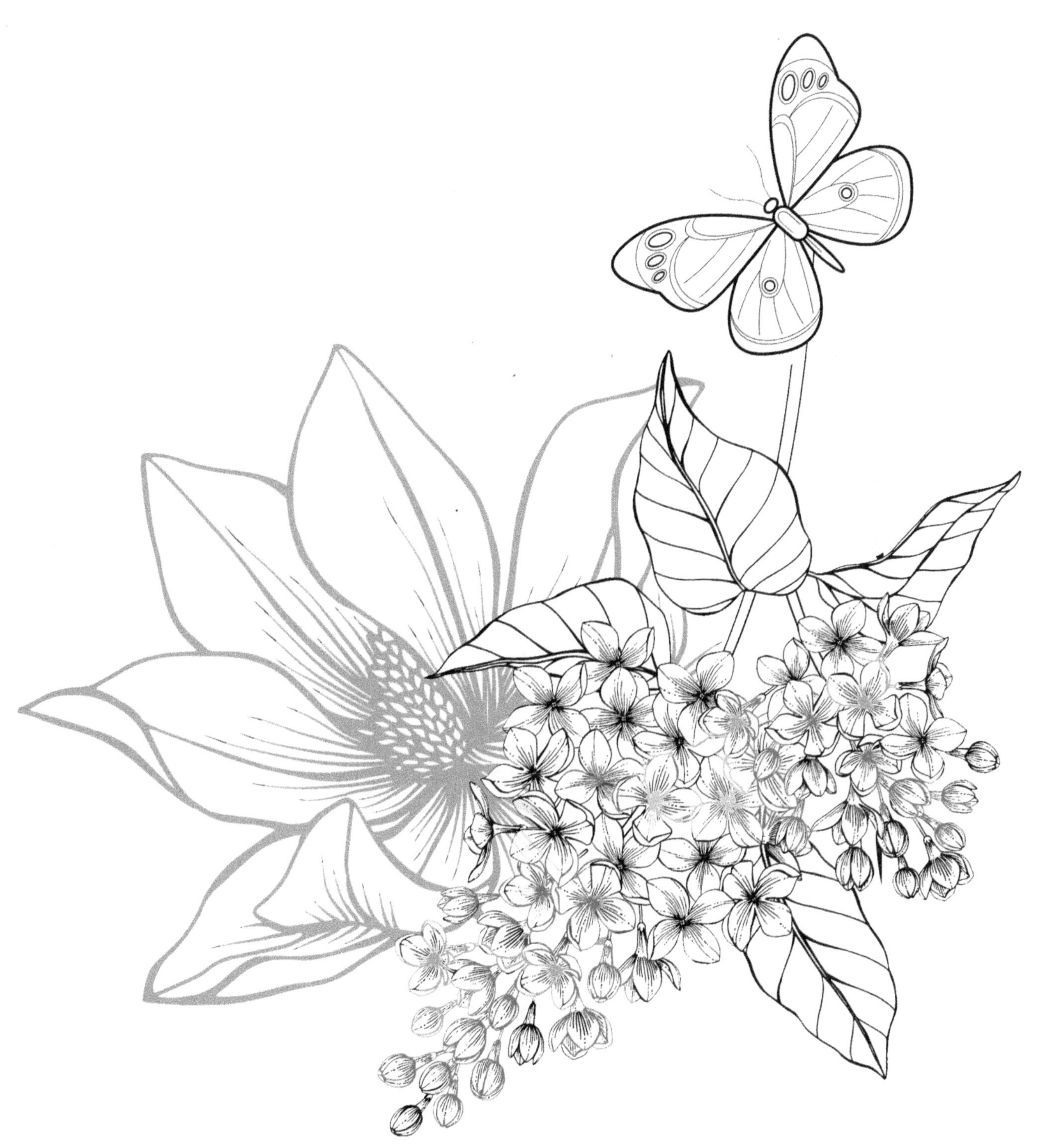

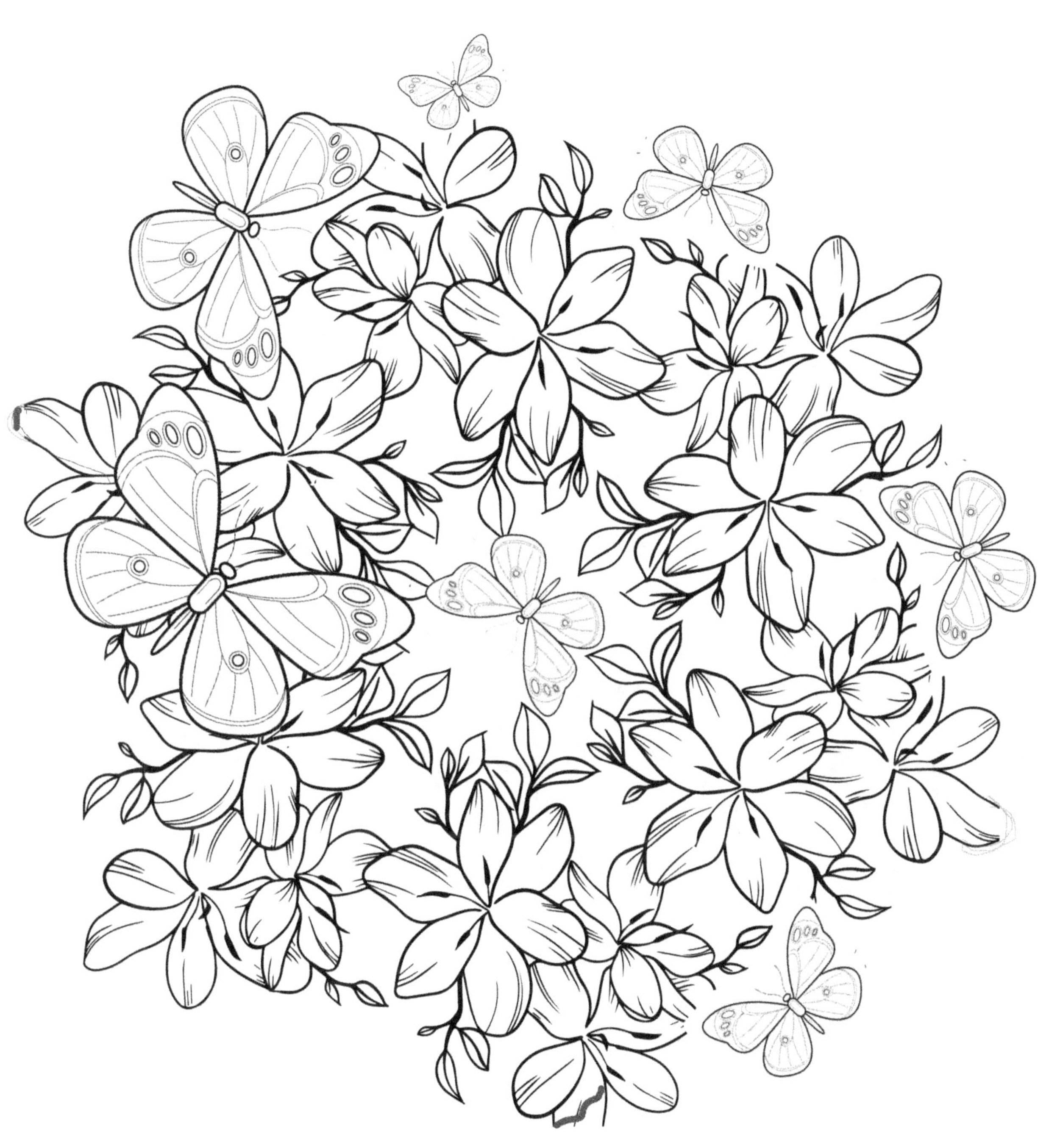

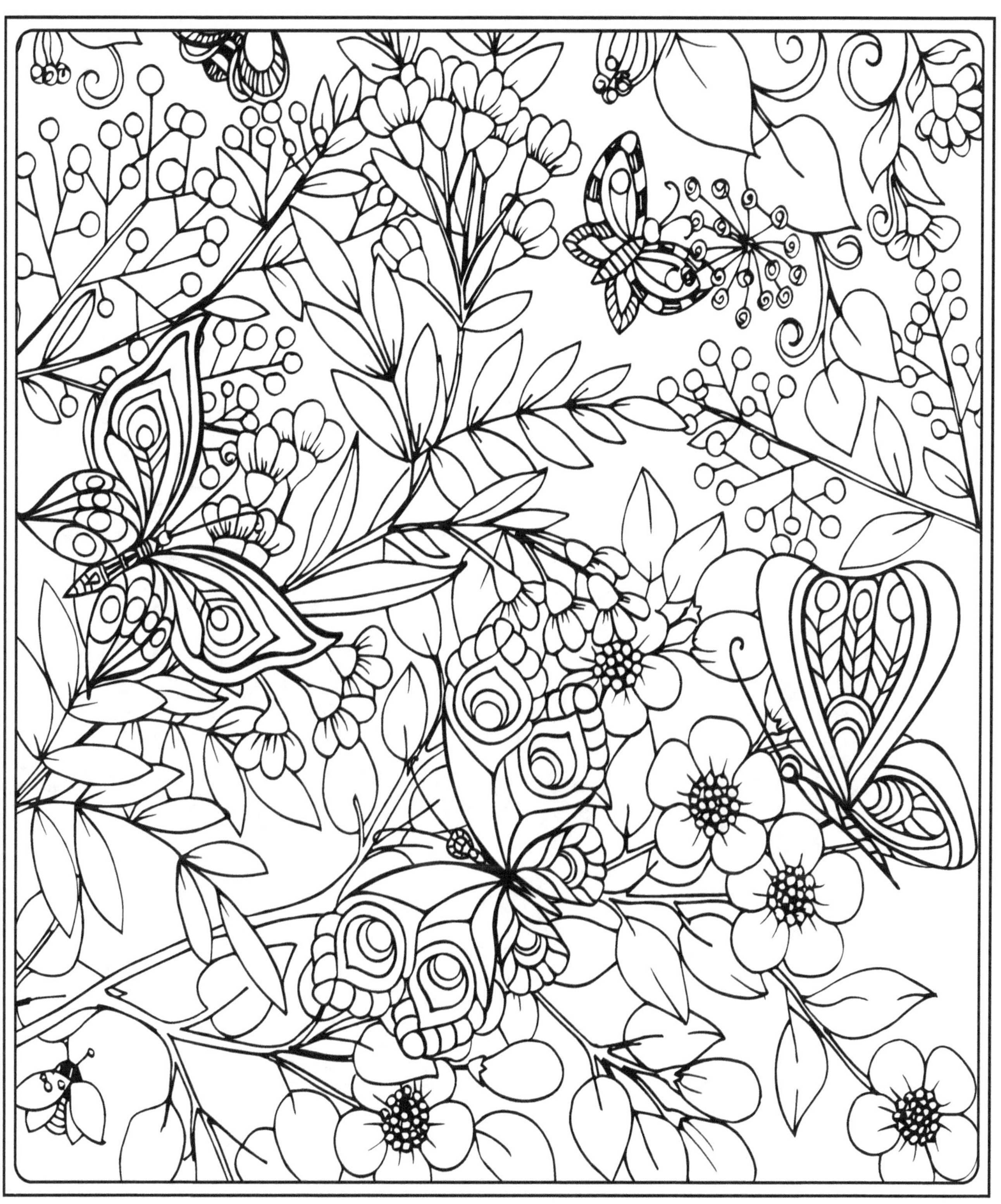

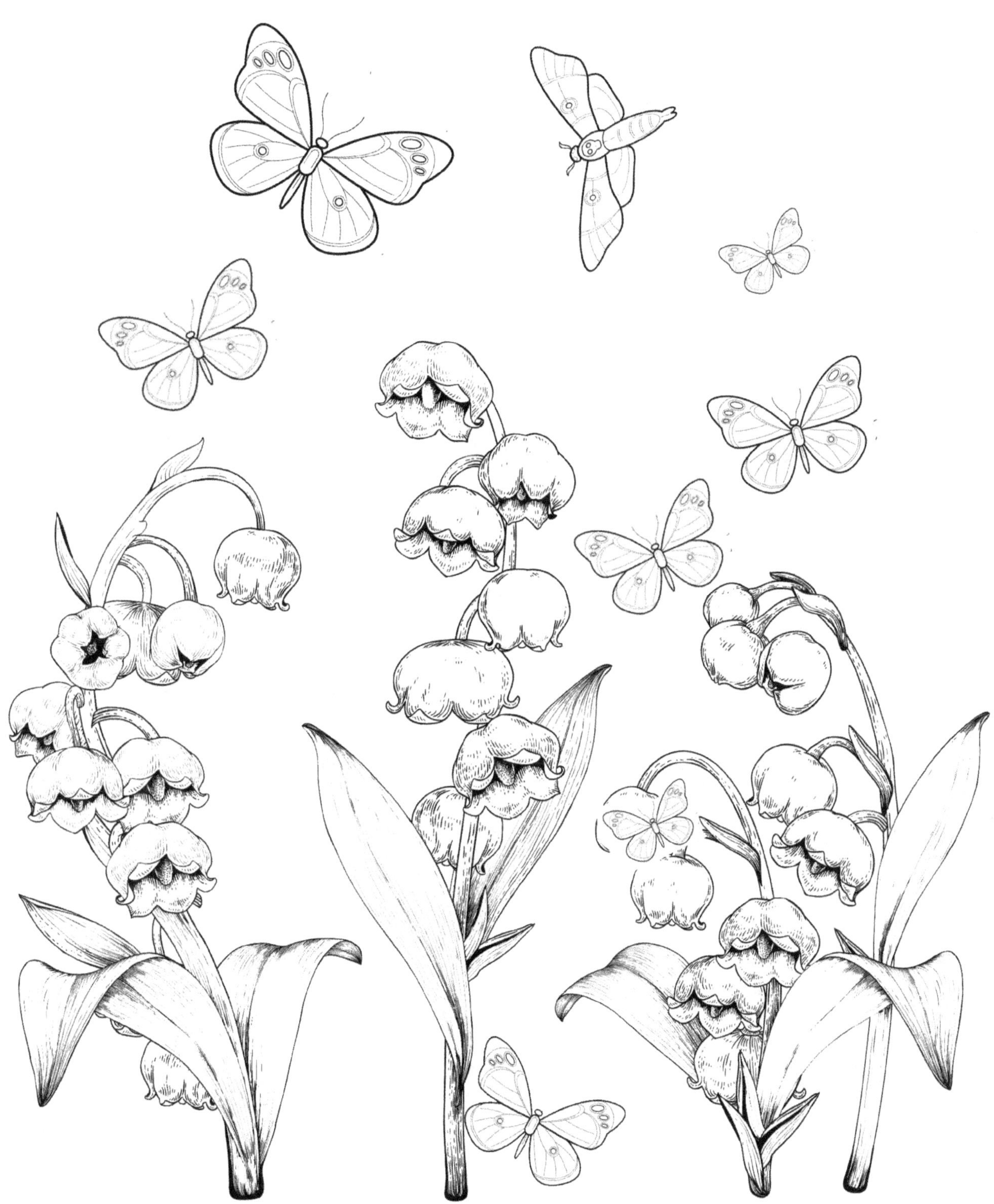

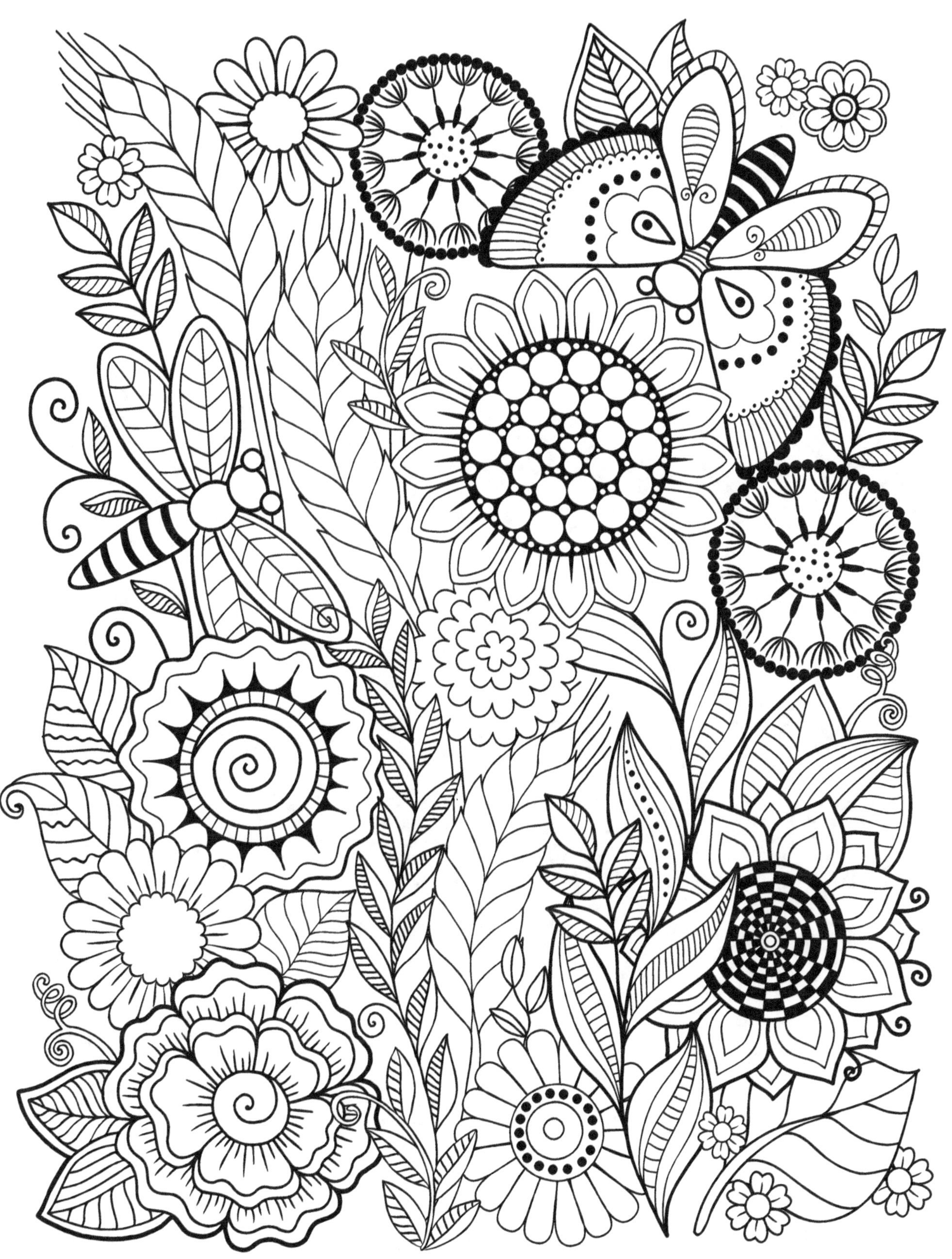

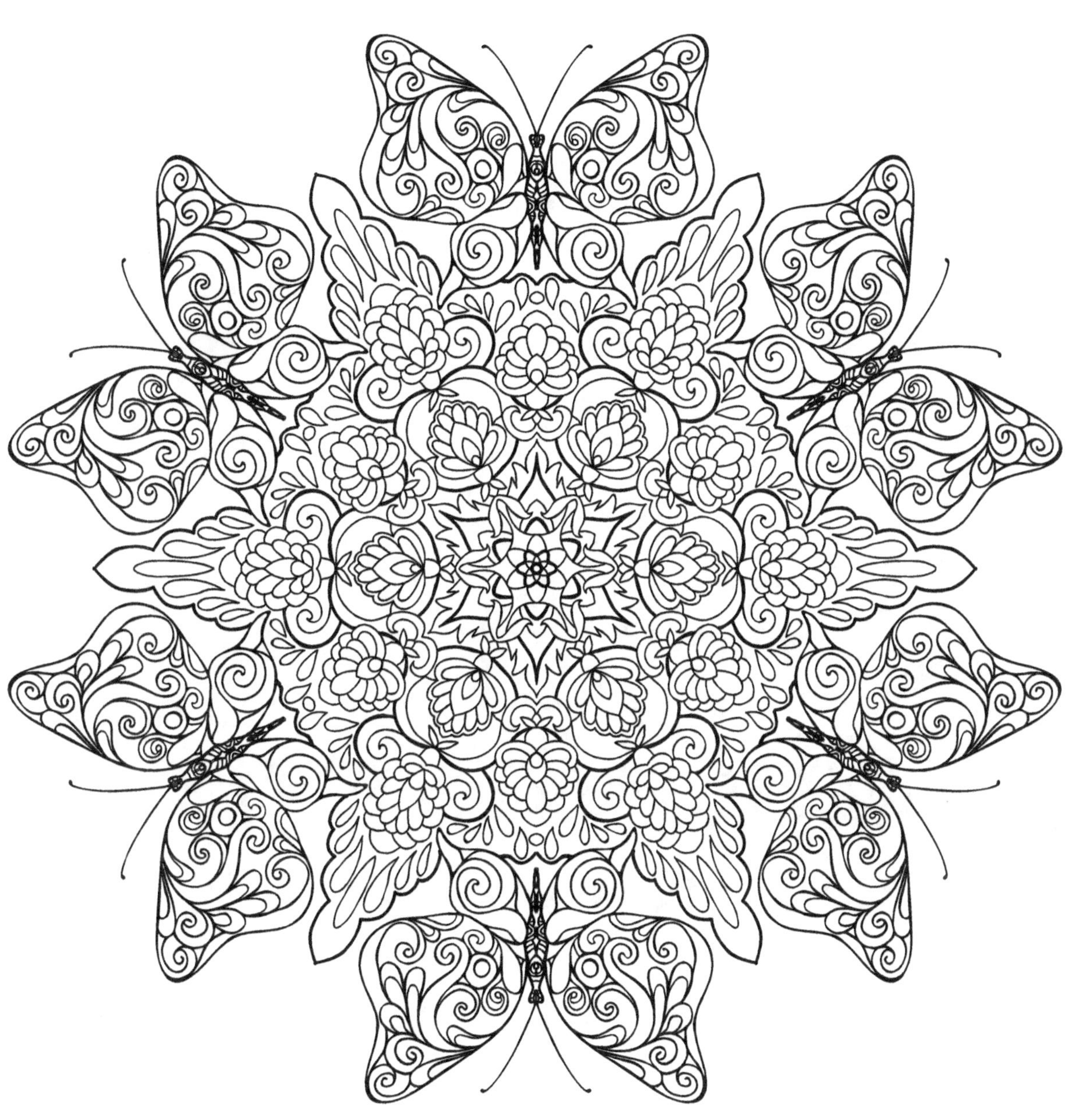

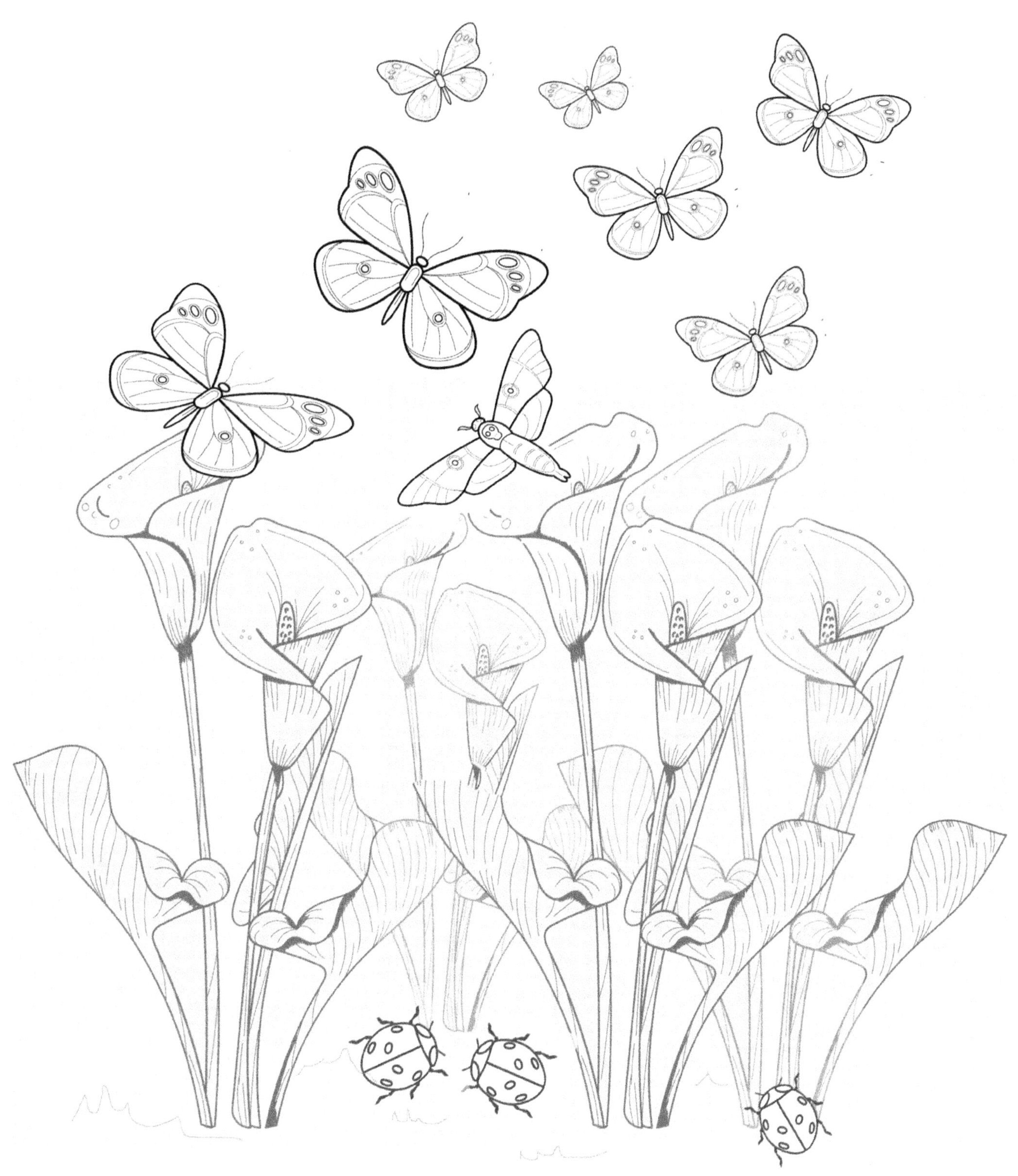

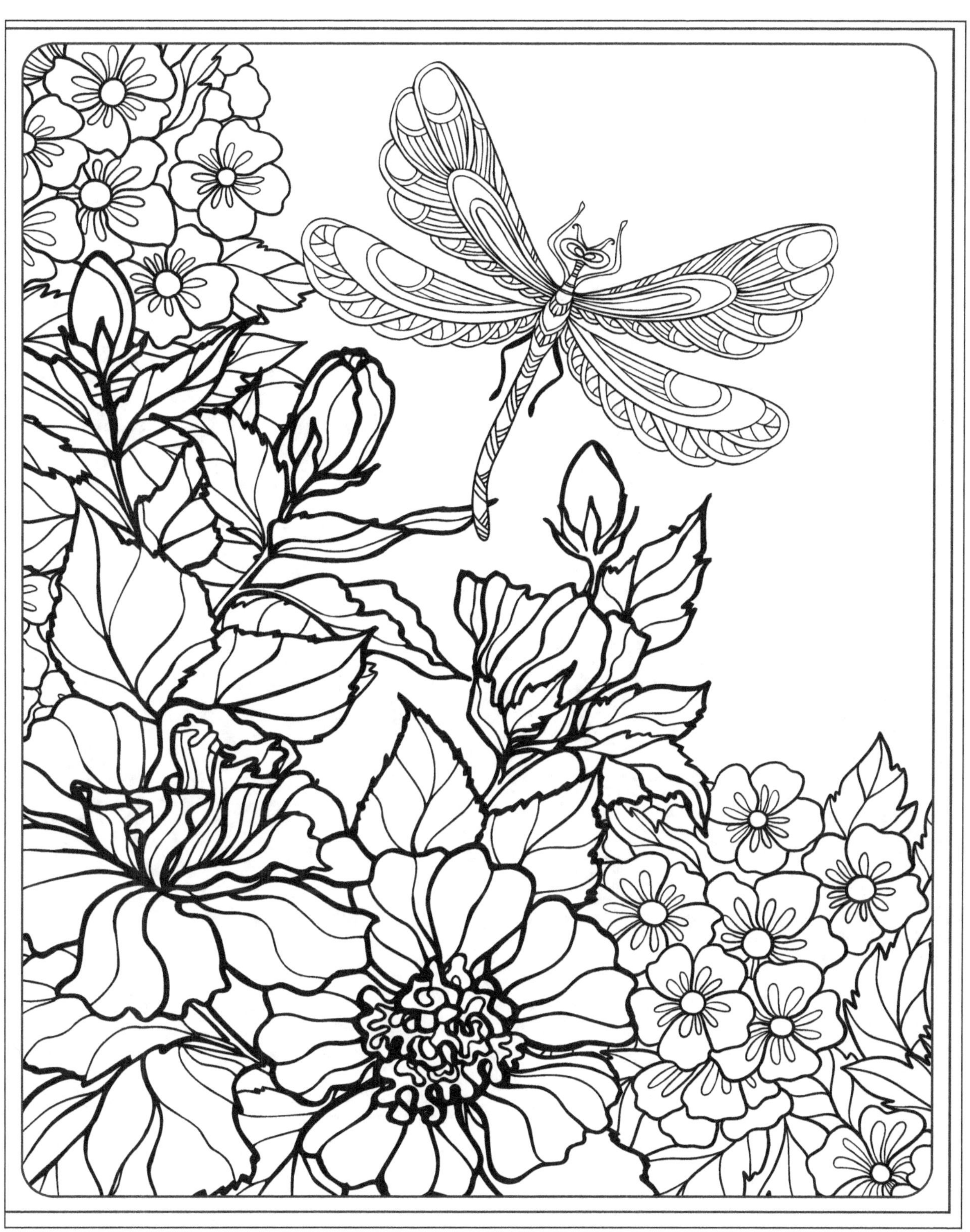

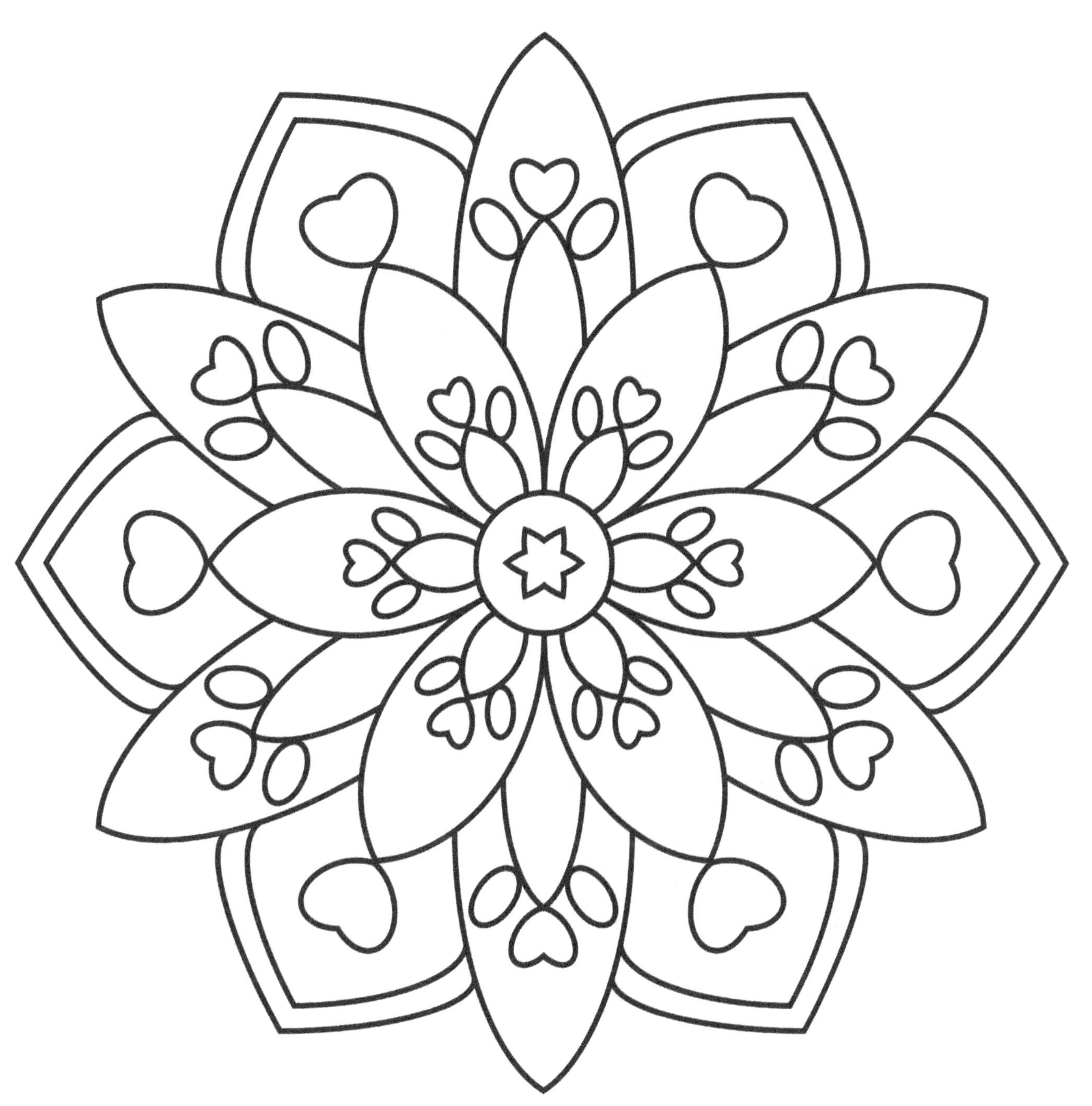

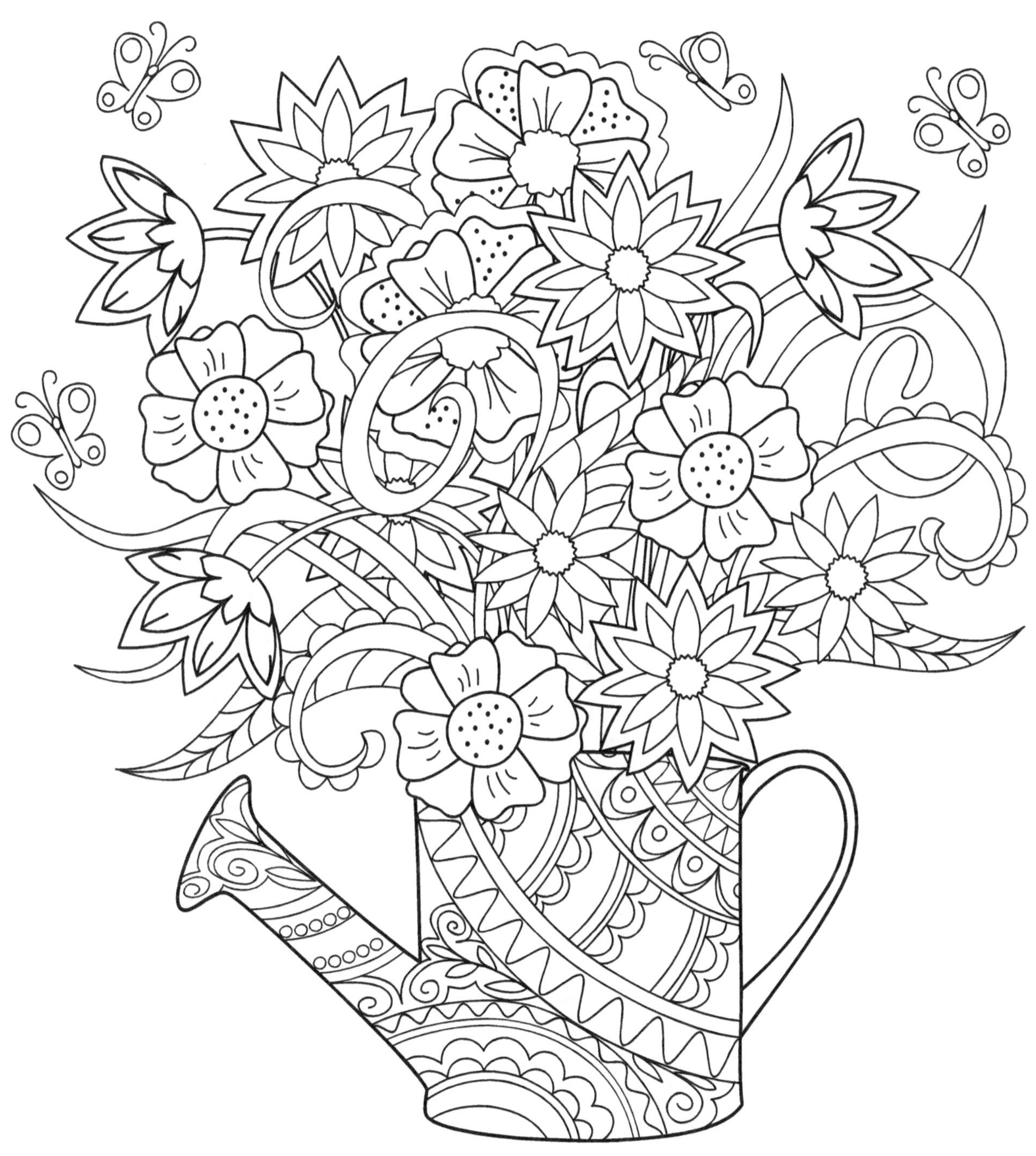

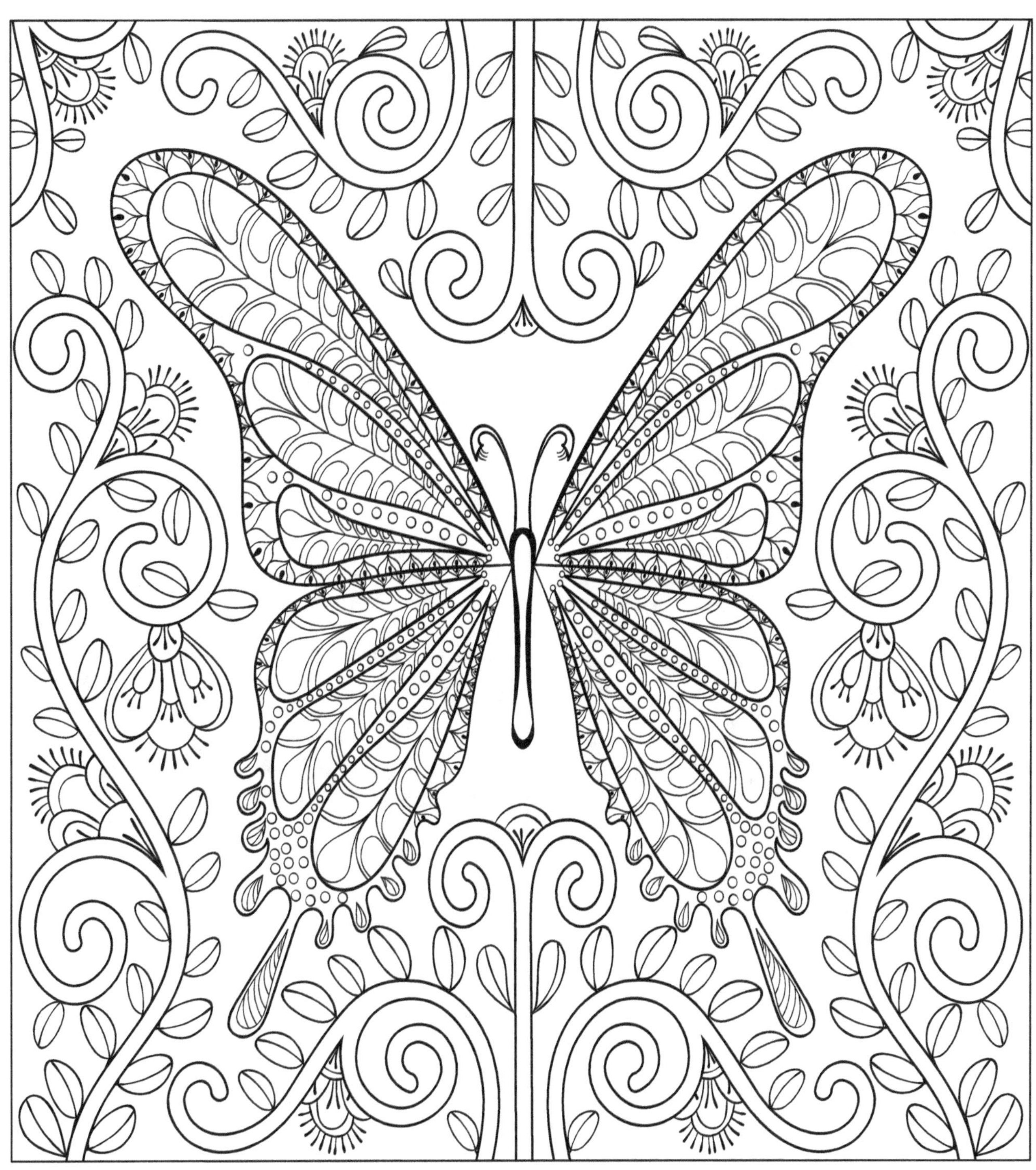

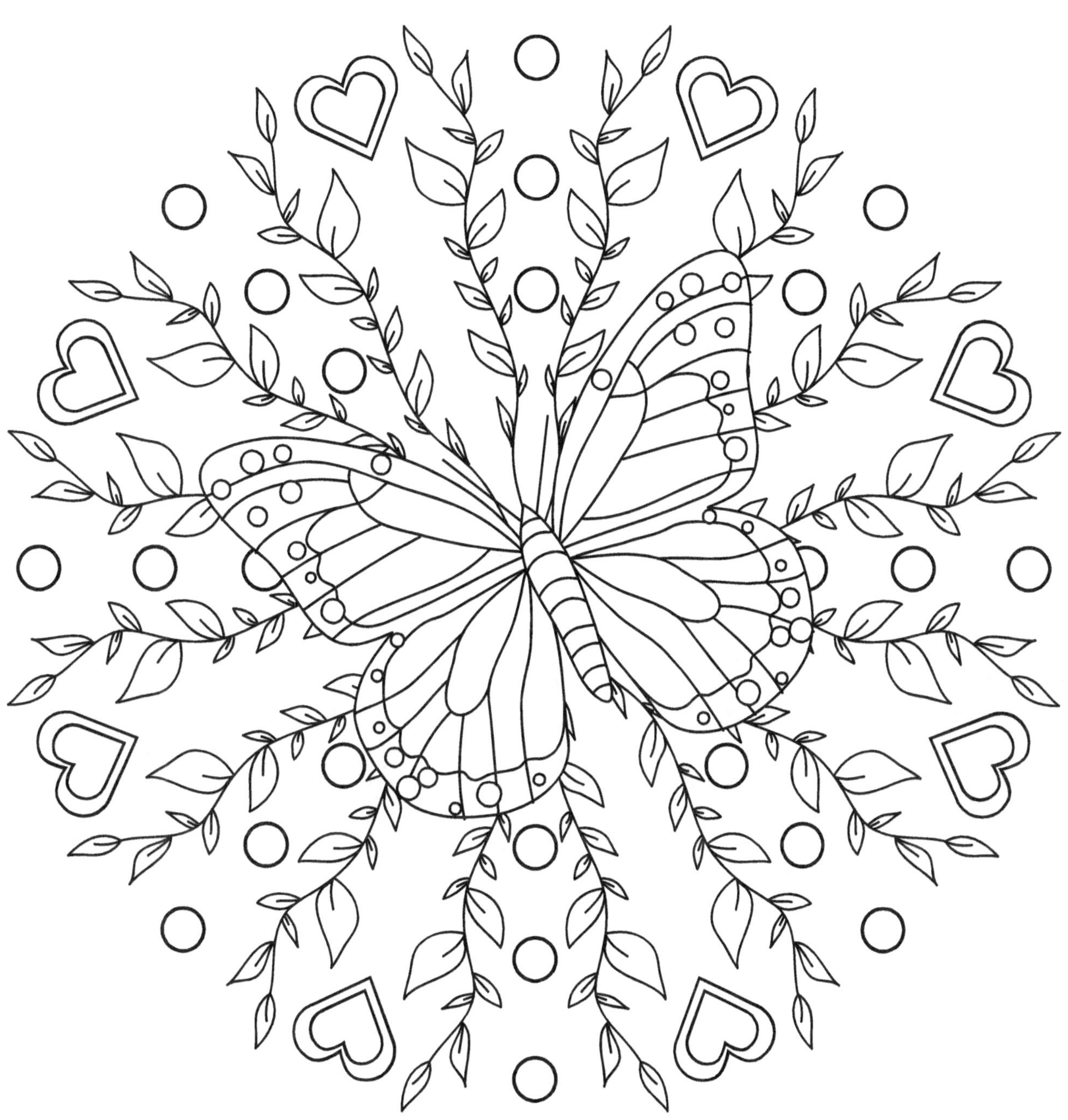

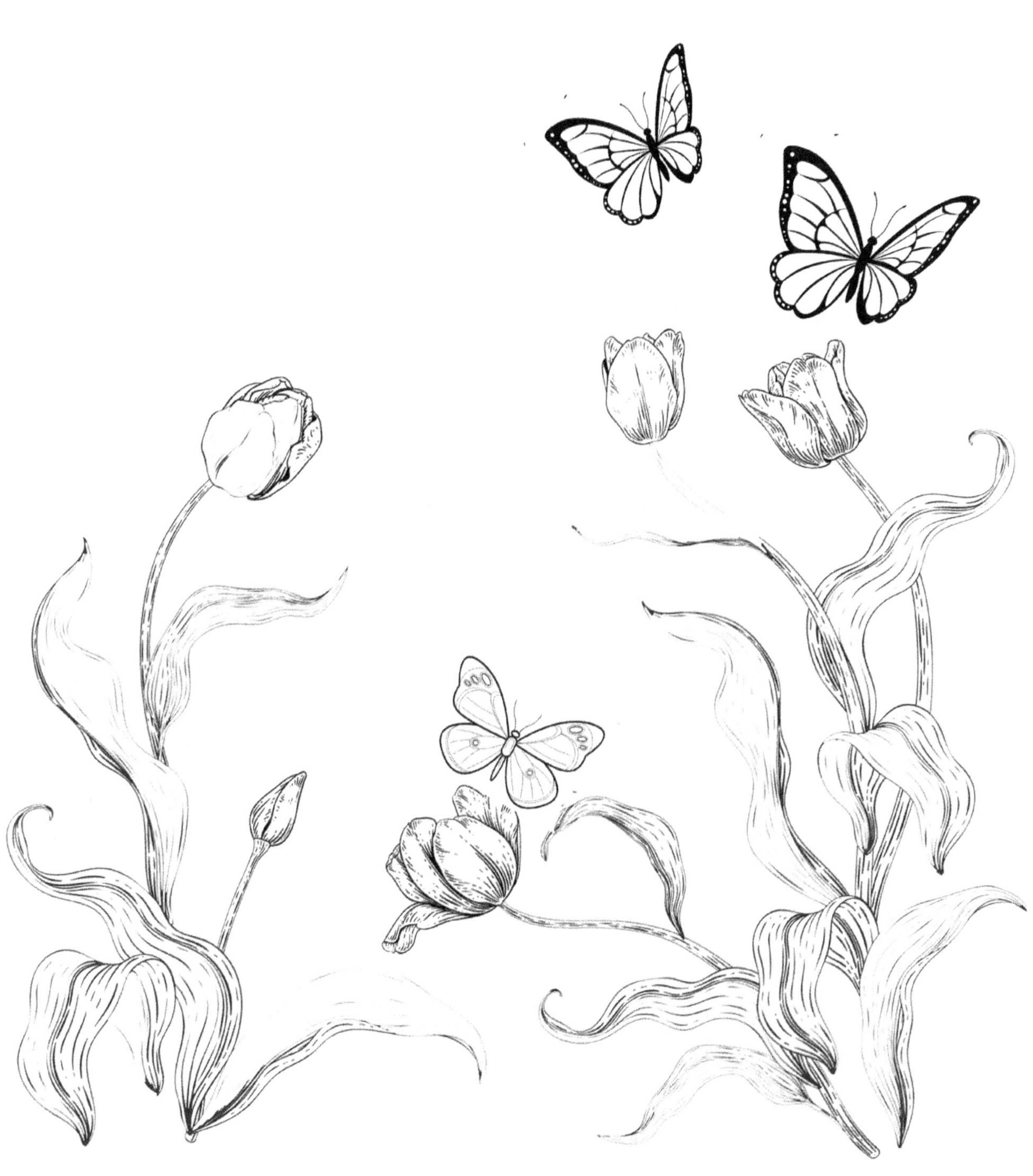

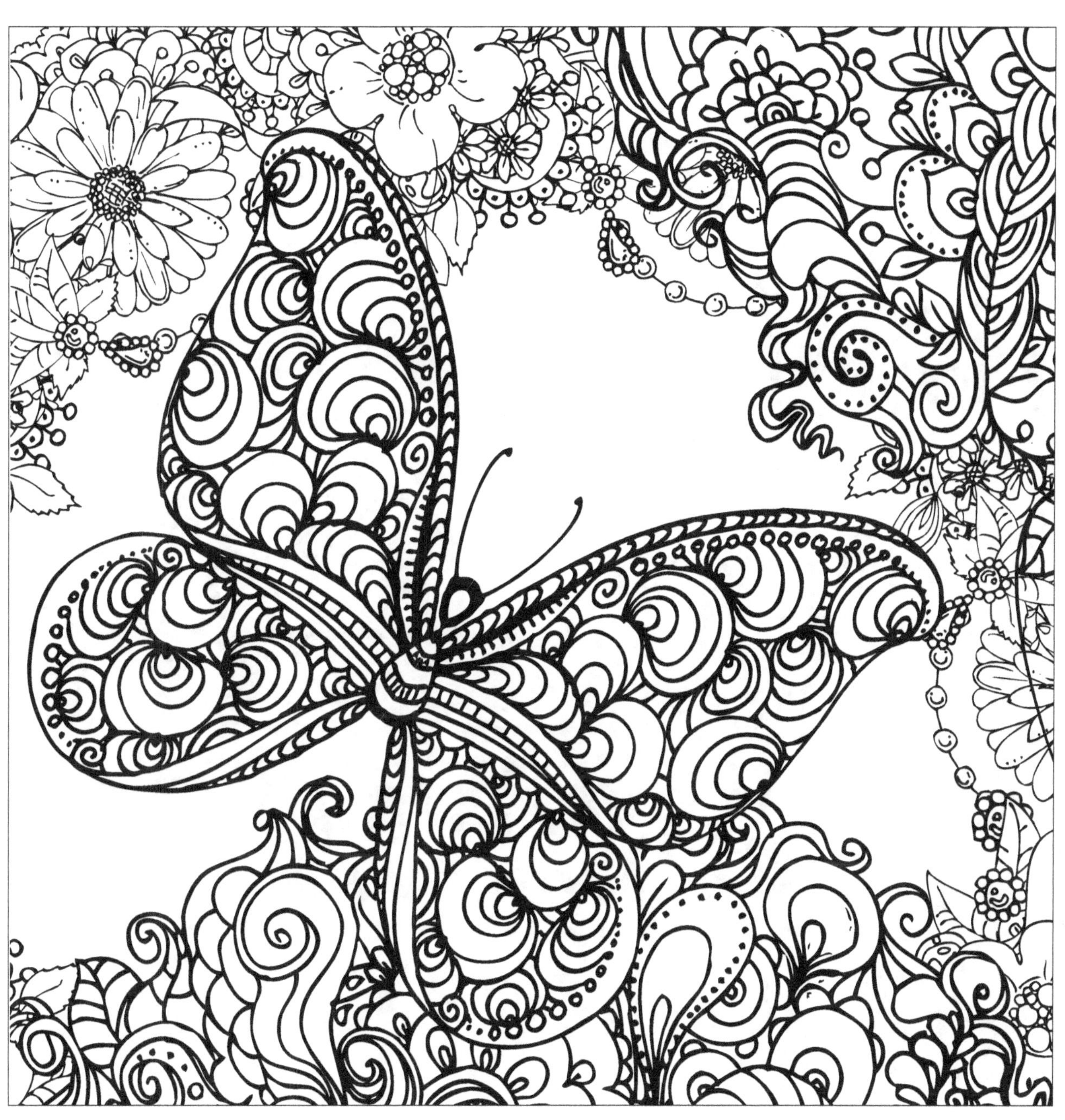

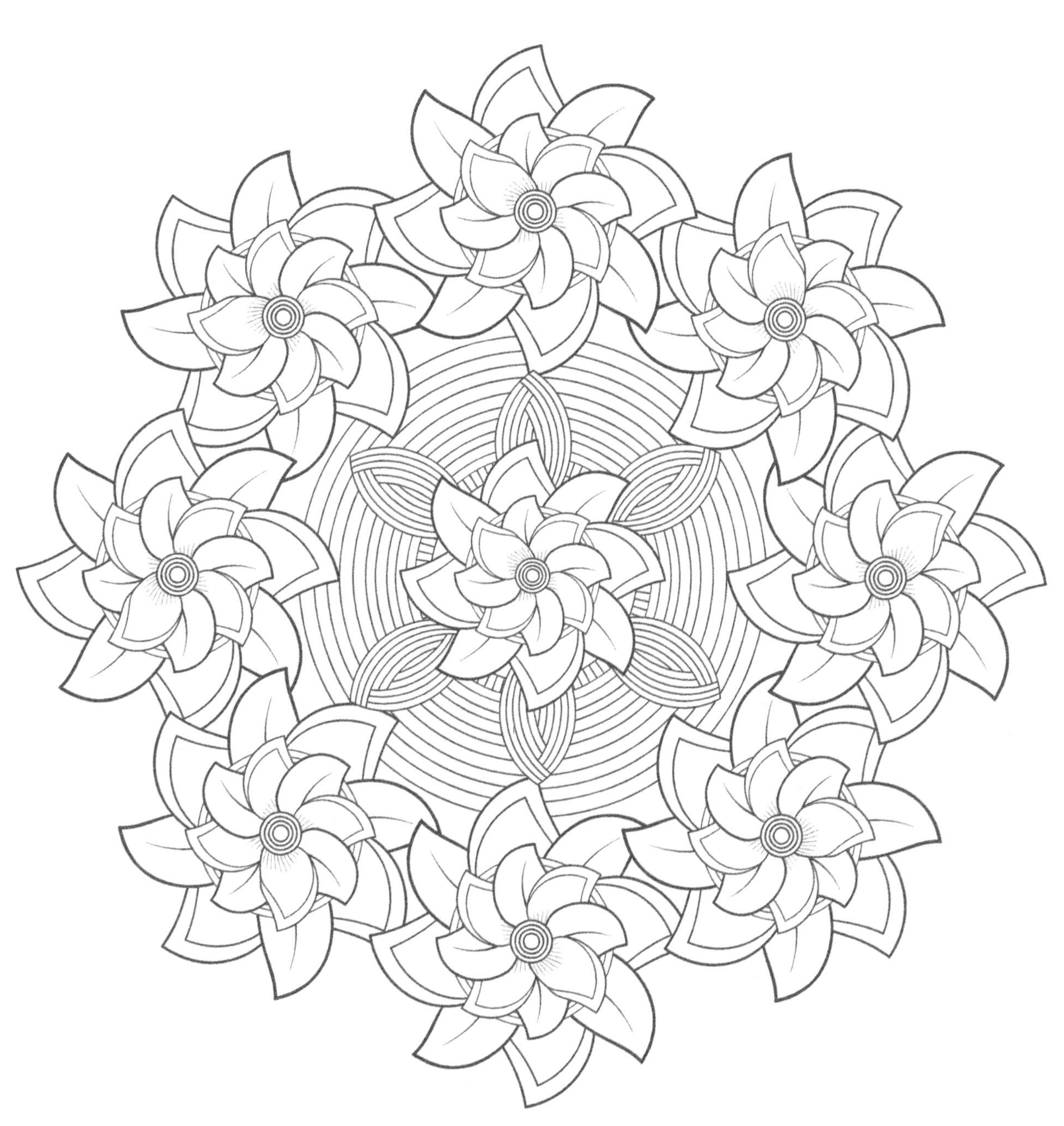

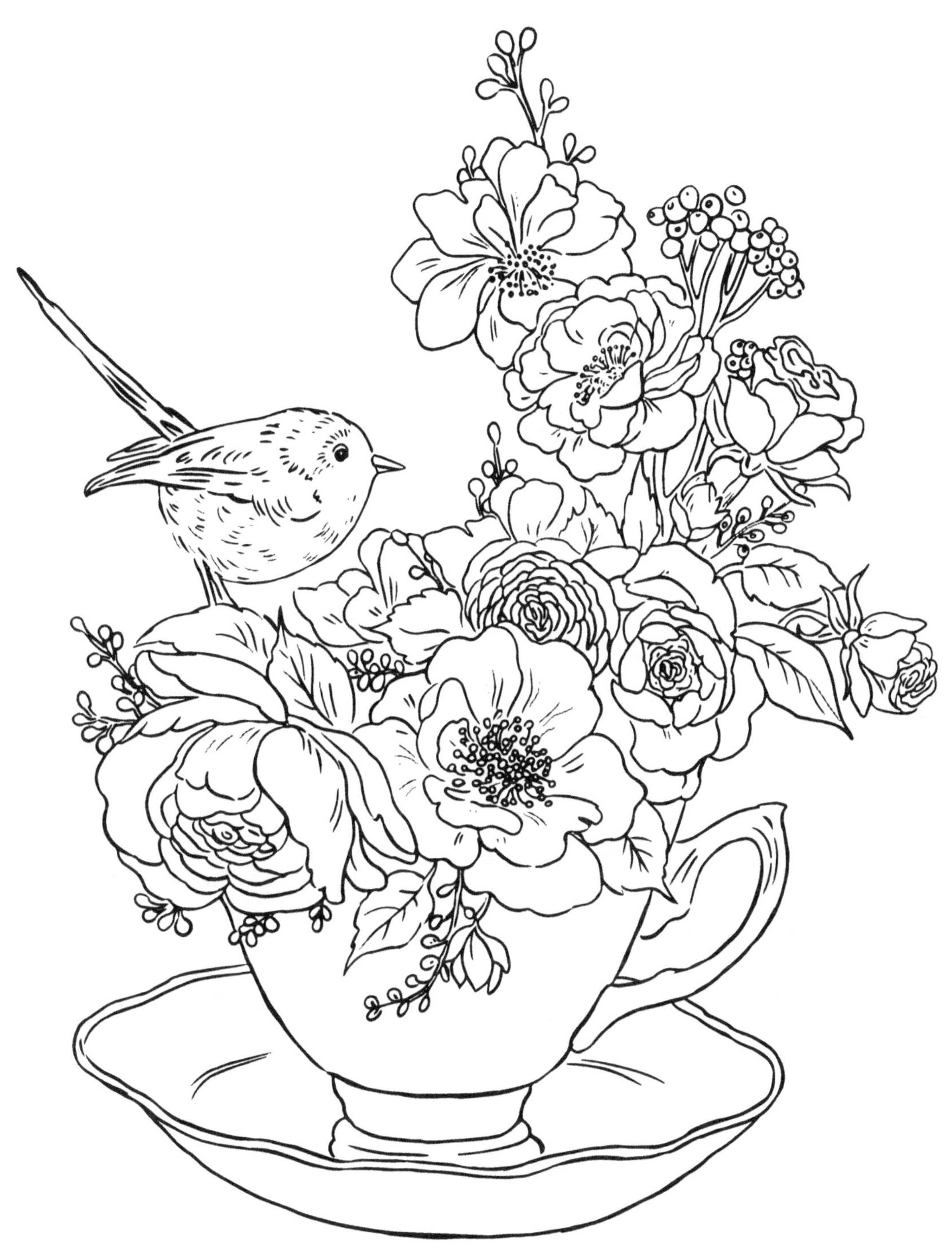

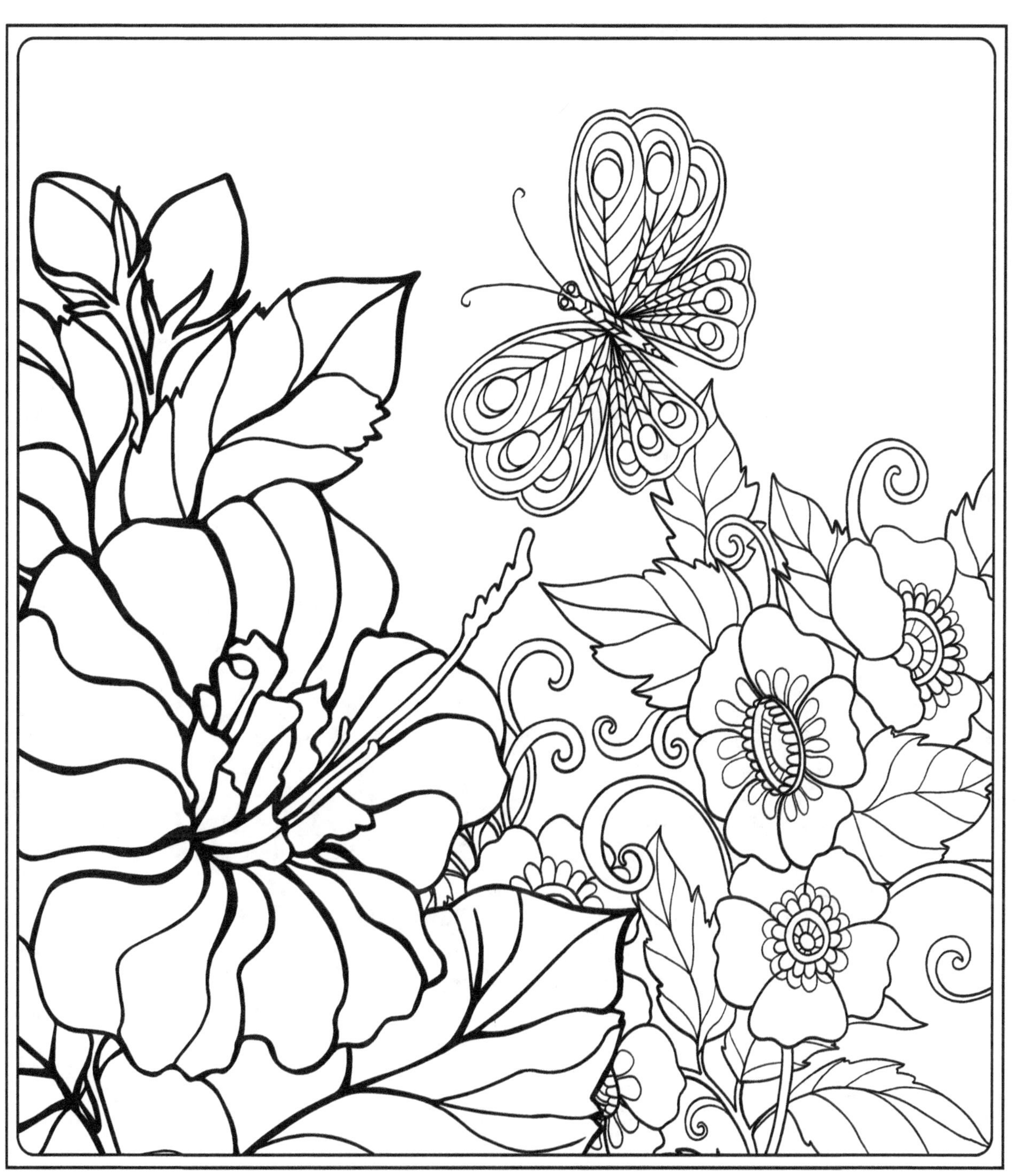

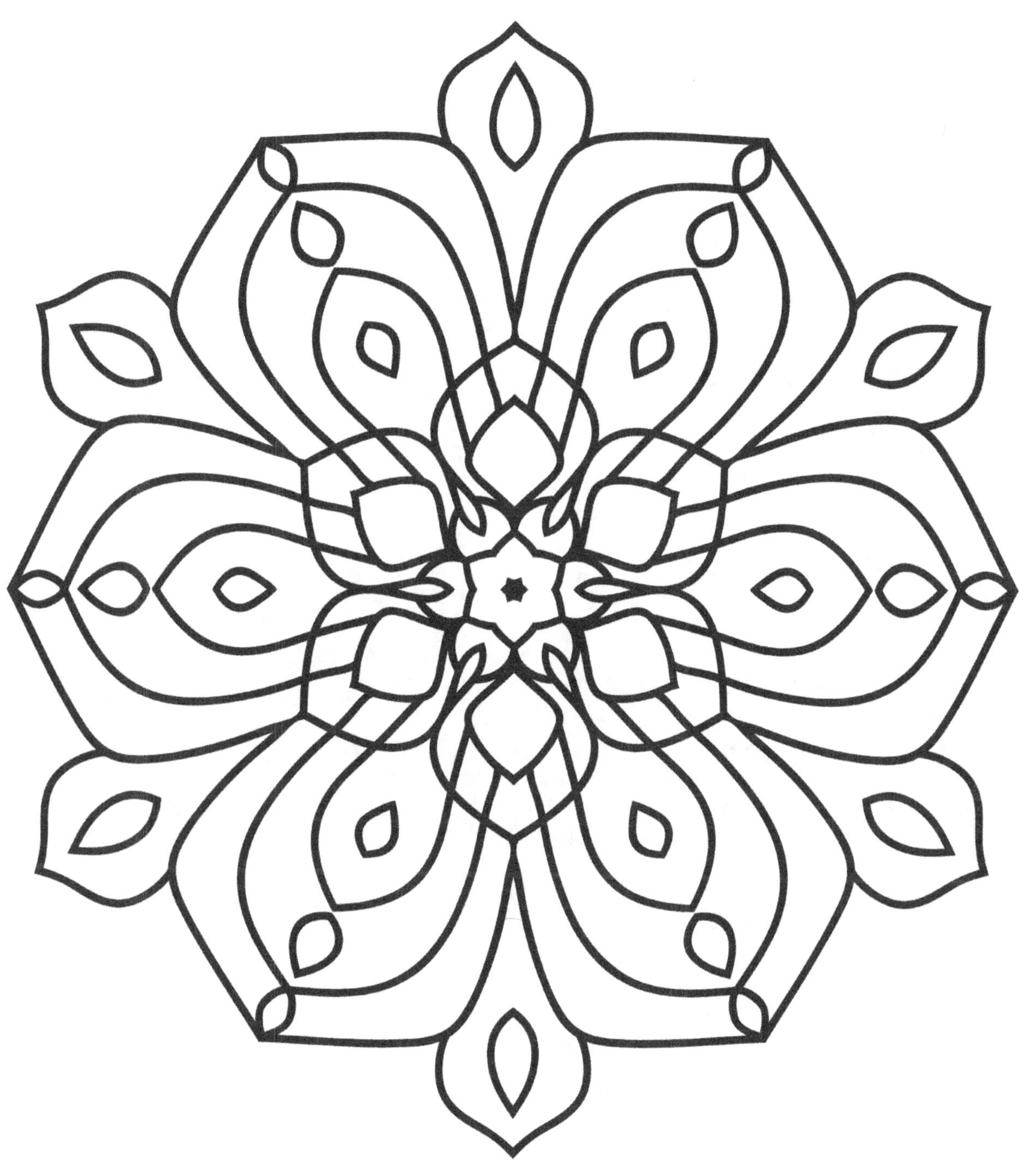

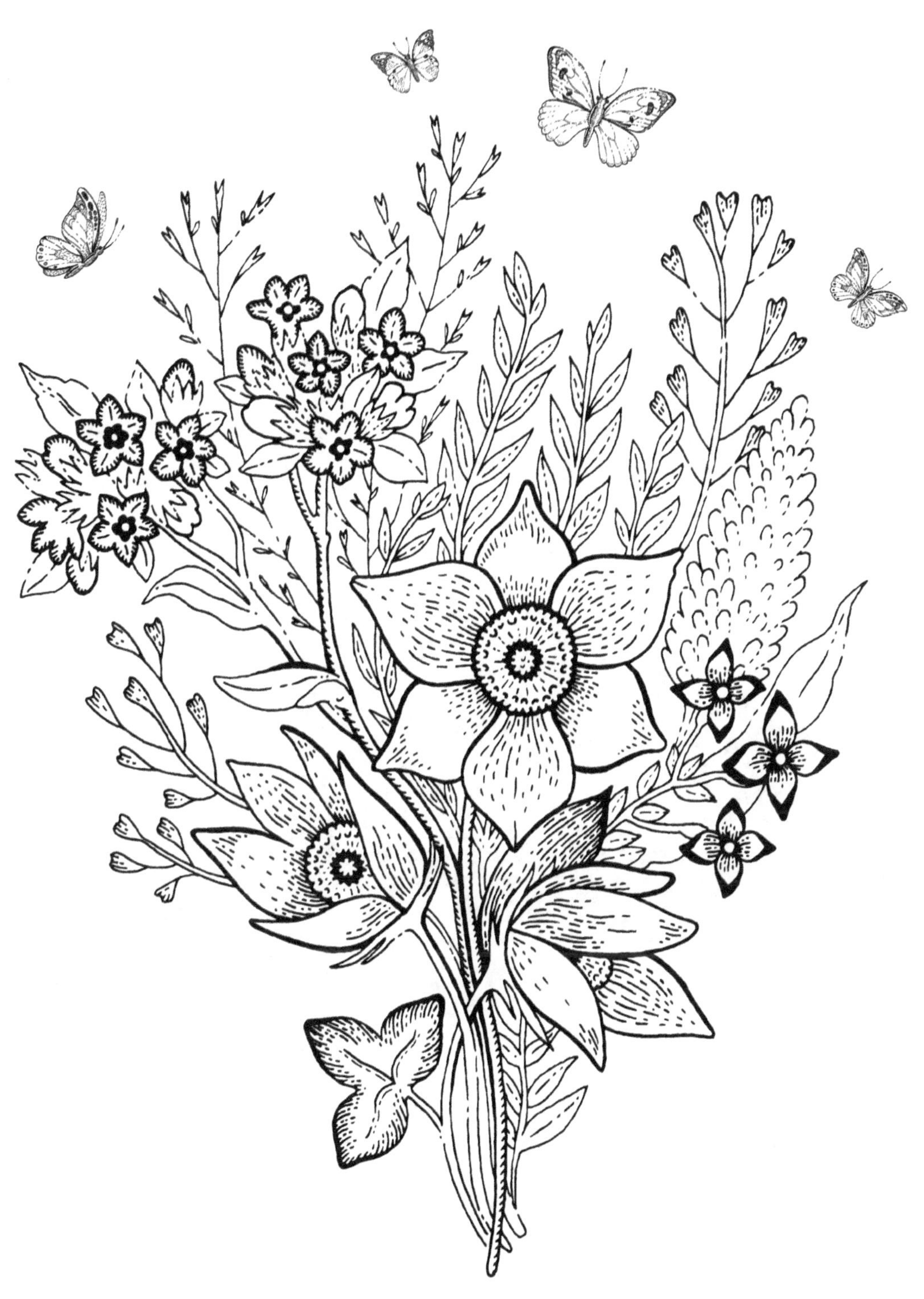

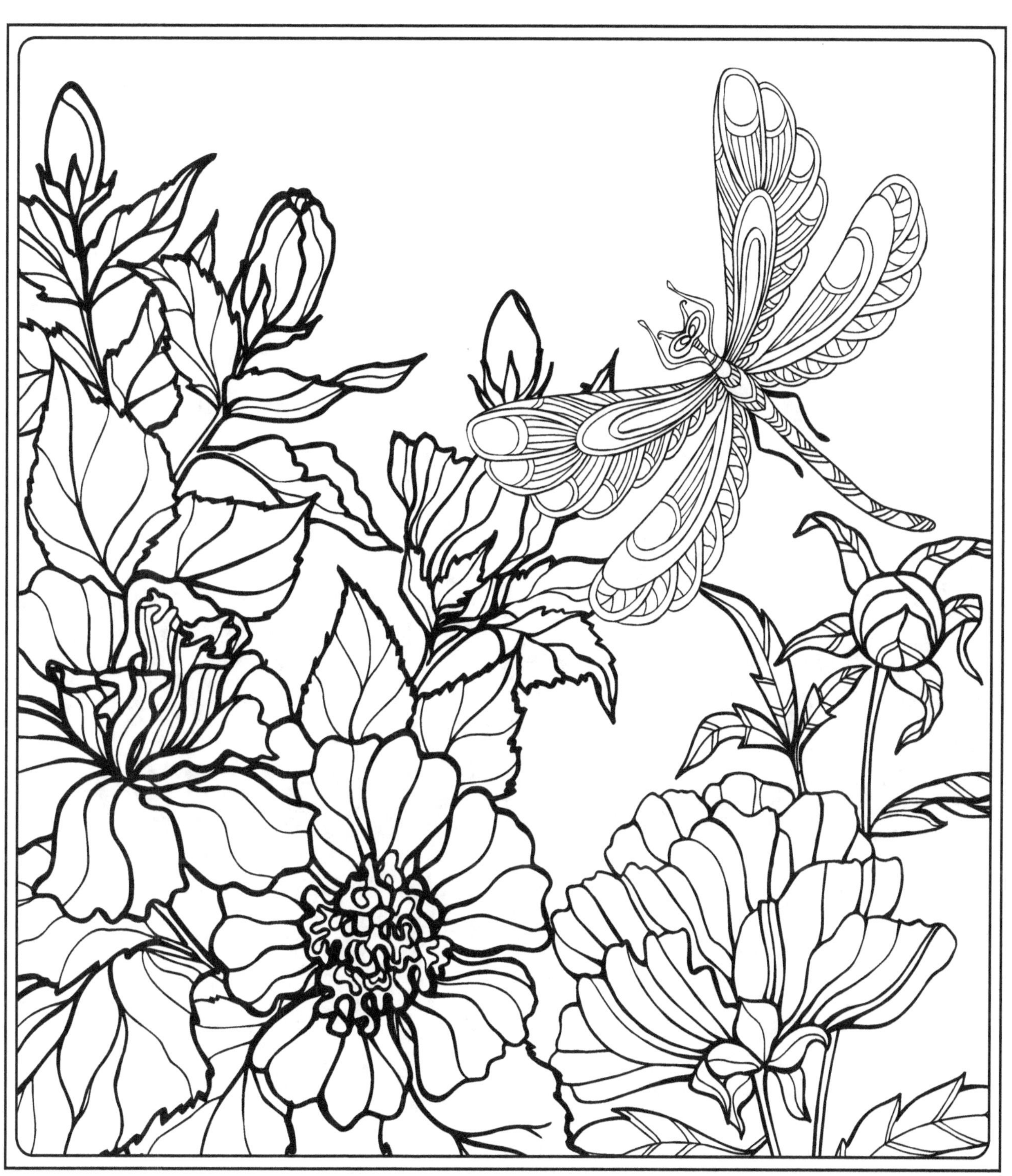

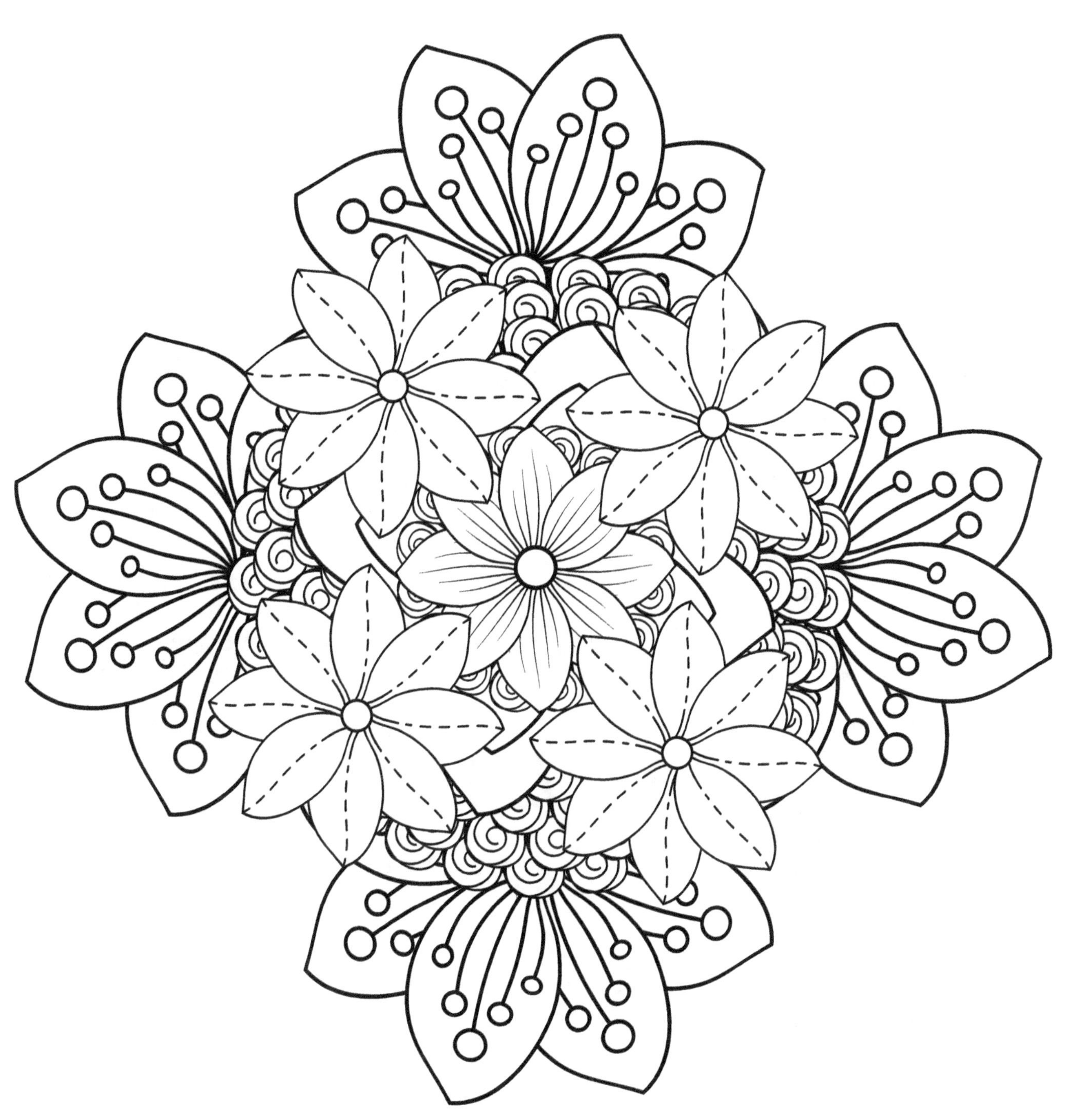

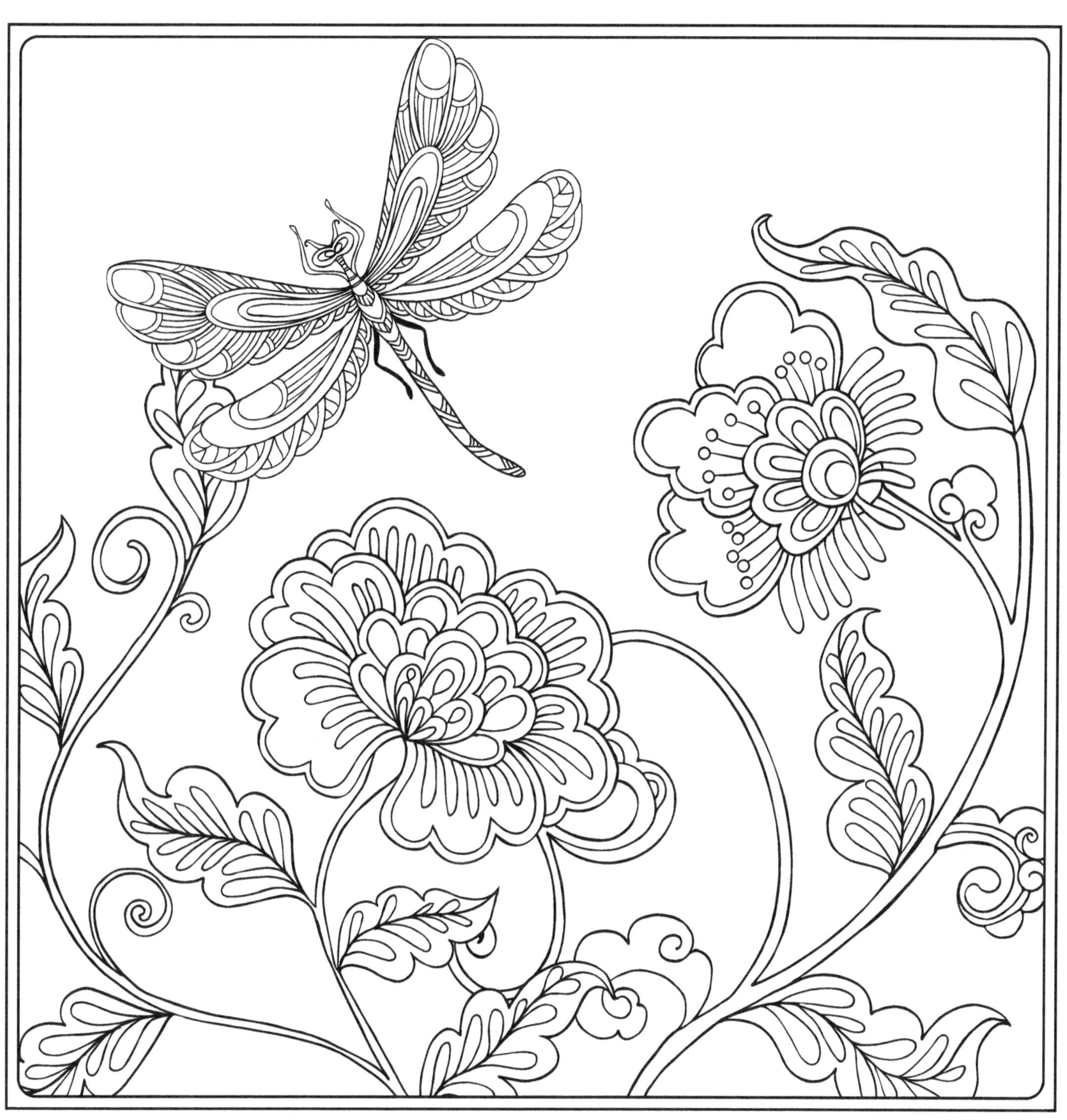

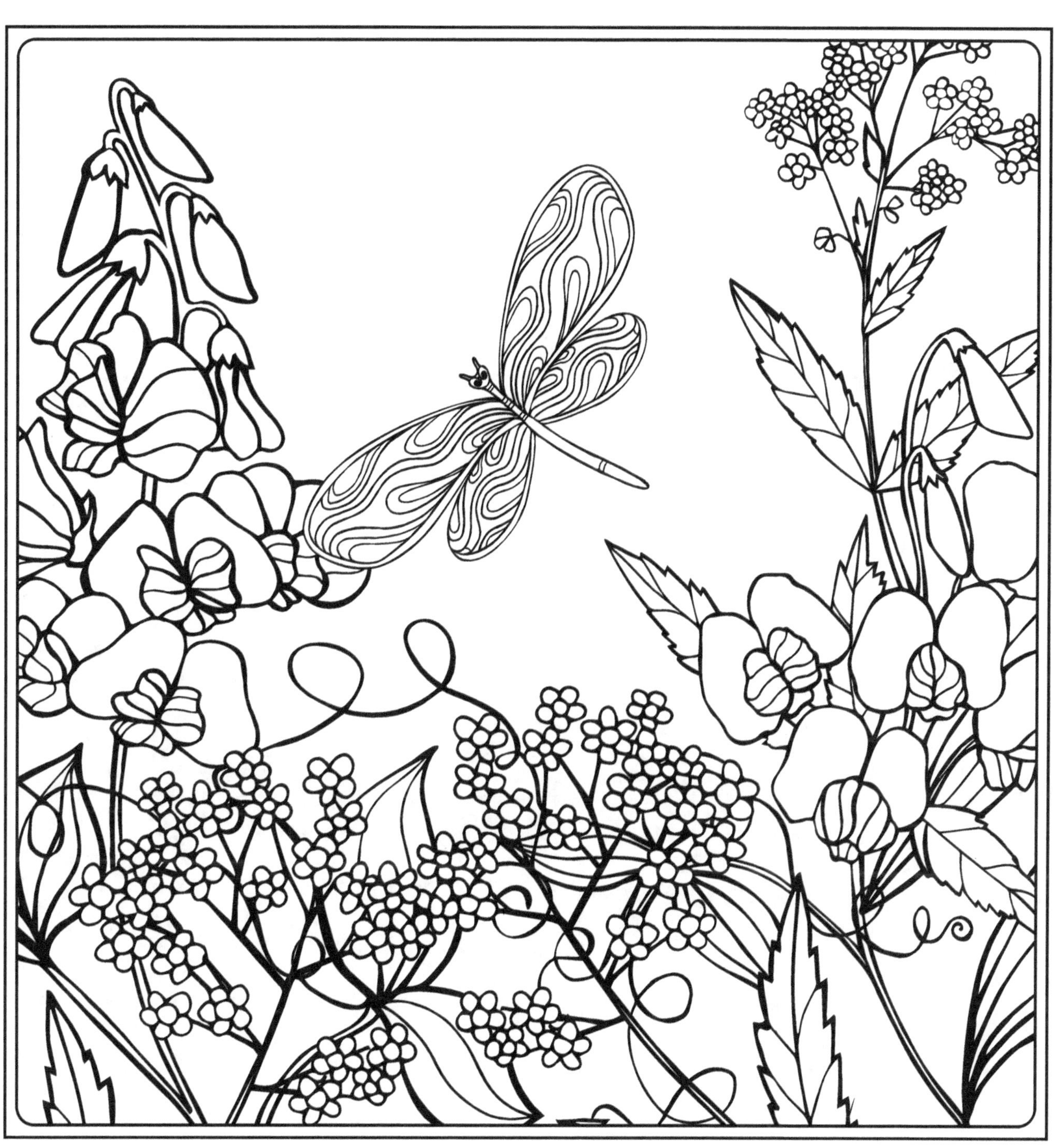

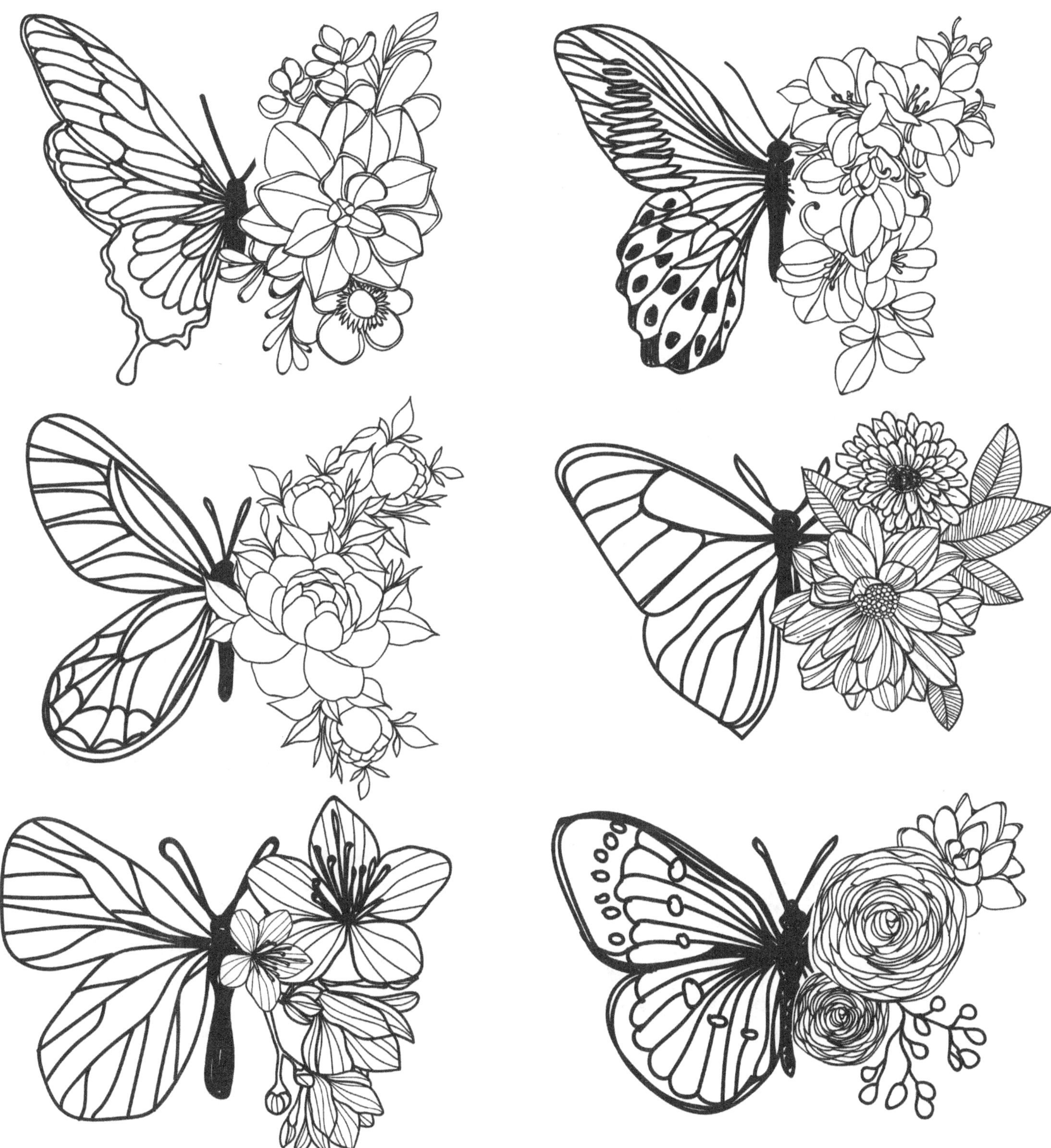

Also available from Annabella Shaw:

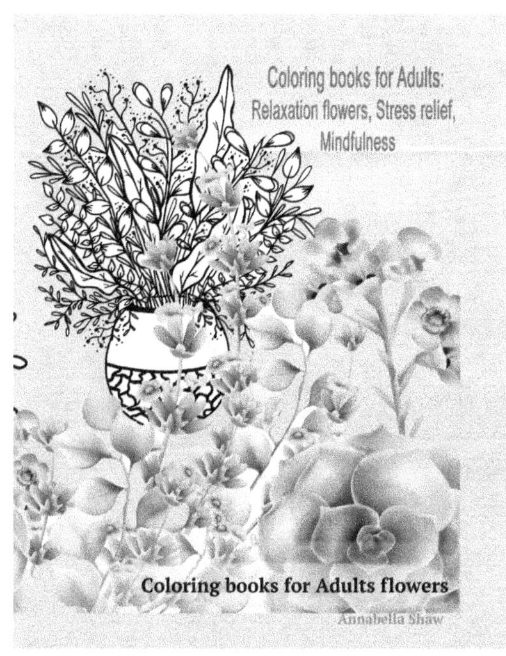

Pretty flower
designs for all
types of abilities.

*Destressing and
Relaxing*

*Coloring books
for Adults
Flowers*

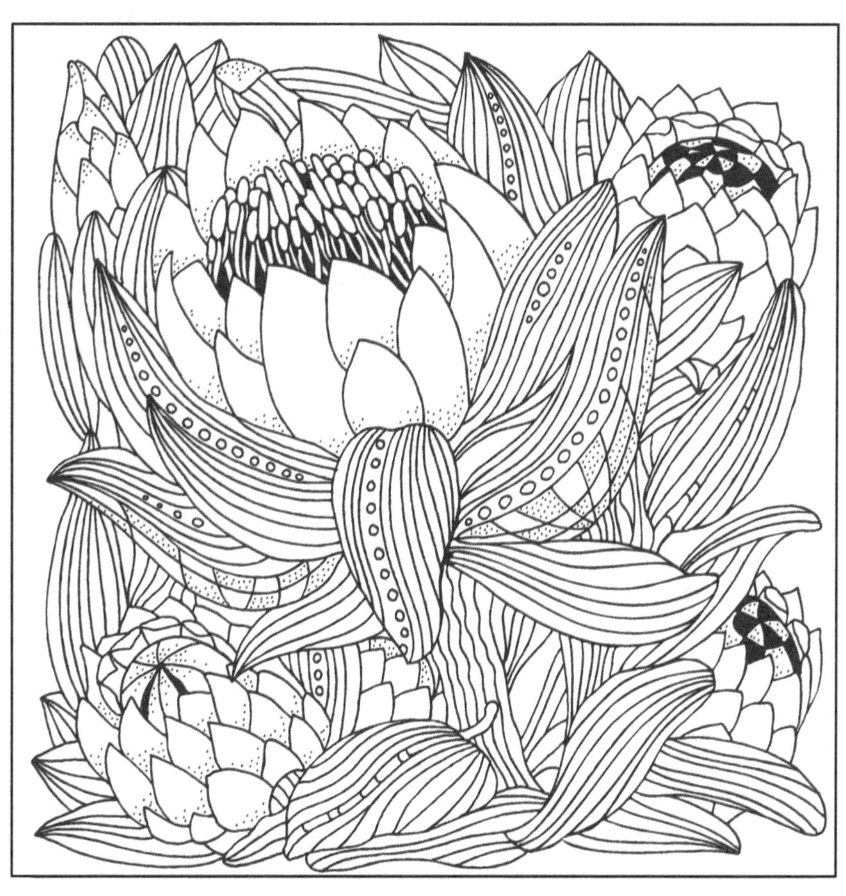

Also available from Annabella Shaw:

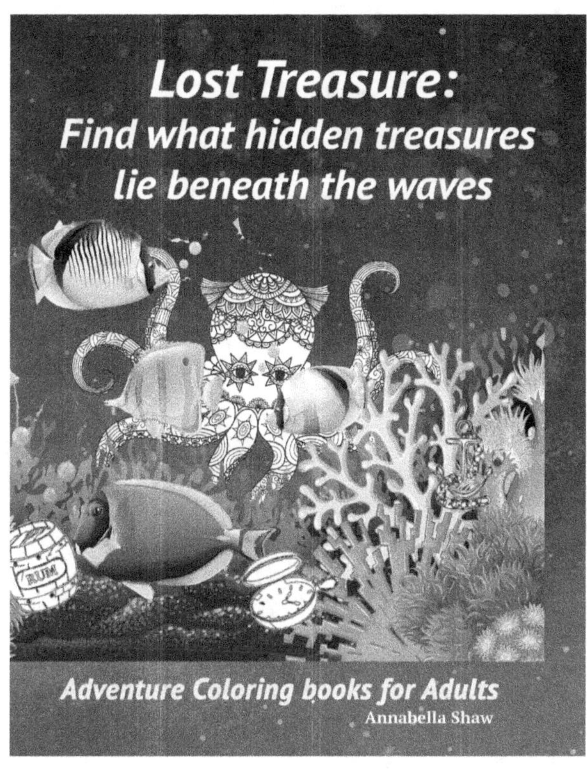

**Lost Treasure:
Adult Adventure
Coloring Book**

Find hidden objects
through beautiful
coloring pages

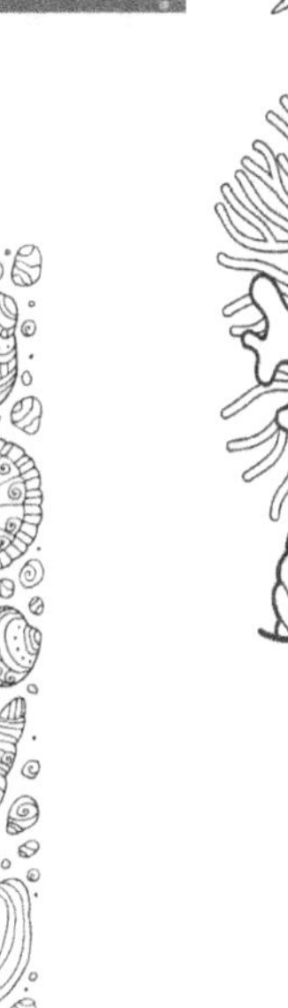

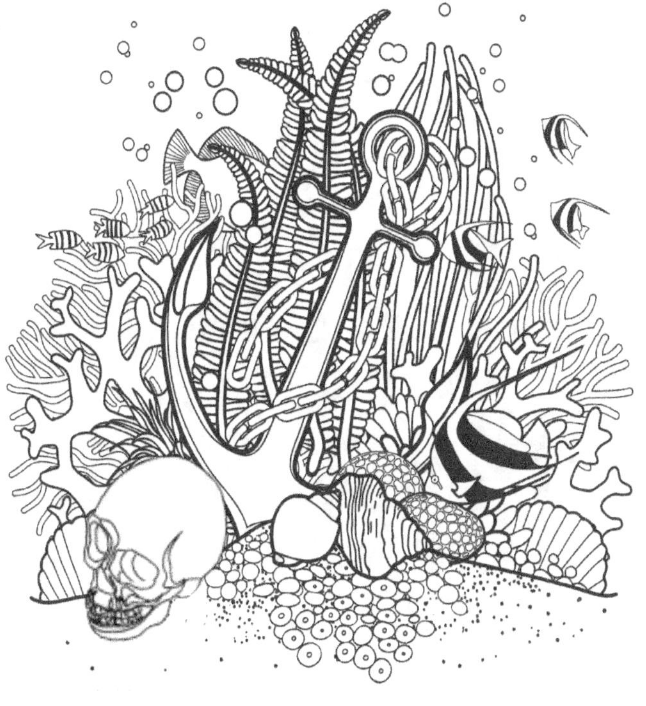

Adventure coloring books for adults

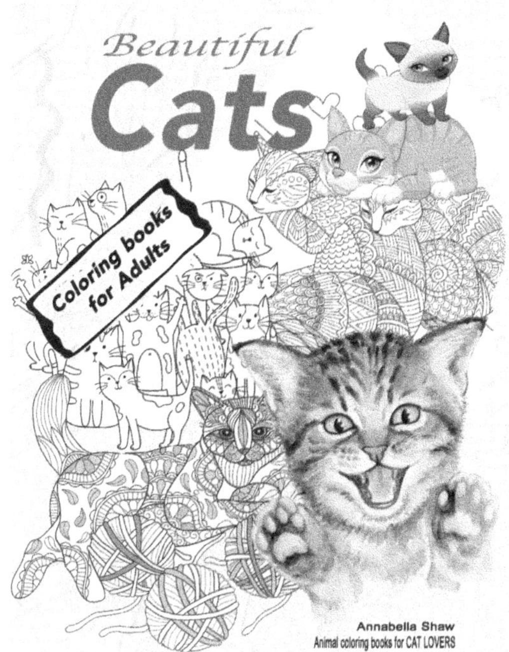

Animal coloring book for CAT LOVERS
Beautiful CAT coloring books for adults

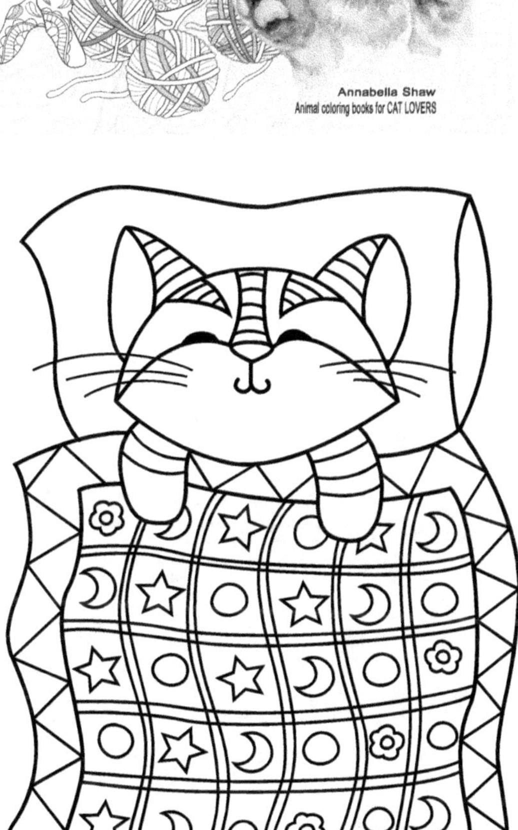

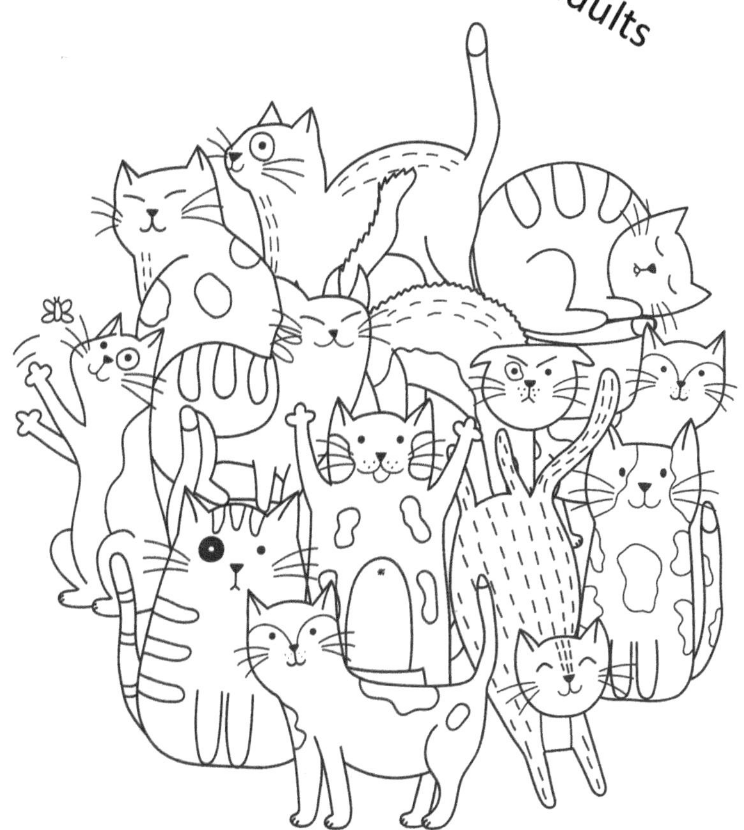

Annabella Shaw

Tag your colored pictures with
#colour_my_art for a change to
get your pictures featured on
our social media